How to Sketch

Contributing Artists

Victor Perard

Genevieve Vaughan-Jackson

Leonard Richmond

Yngve Edward Soderberg

Rune Hagman

A GD/PERIGEE BOOK

Perigee Books
are published by
The Putnam Publishing Group
200 Madison Avenue
New York, New York 10016

ISBN 0-399-50951-8
Library of Congress catalog card number: 60-13318

First Perigee printing, 1983
Four previous Grosset & Dunlap printings
Printed in the United States of America
     5 6 7 8 9

FIRST OF ALL

Art is the finest way of doing anything. Pencil, pen and ink, and charcoal drawings are among the fine arts. The student should master these techniques.

It is important to have the right tools to work with: a medium hard pencil (H. B.), a medium soft pencil (2B), and a soft eraser for pencil drawings. India ink can be used with a pen or brush in various shades. The brushes which should be used are from No. 1 up. A No. 6 round brush with sable bristles is perhaps the most useful. The pen most frequently used is a croquil. Charcoal (or carbon pencil) is often a good thing for a beginner to use. It comes in varying degrees of hardness. Use a medium stick or pencil at first.

Materials should be treated with respect. Learn to use your pencils deftly with varying pressures to obtain the dark and light tones. Keep your drawing neat; aim at a professional appearance.

Before starting to draw, analyze your subject carefully. Ask yourself what are the principal lines of action. Study the proportions, that is, the length and width compared with the height. Observe from which side of your subject the light is coming. Shadows occur where the rays of light are withheld by the protruding form of the subject. You make use of the shadows to give depth and thickness, and by varying the intensity of the tints, you give the impression of the subject as it appears to the eyes.

Once you have analyzed the subject you intend to draw, the next step is to consider the proper placing of the drawing on the page. To do this, sketch with your finger on the paper an *imaginary* outline of the picture; at the same time try to visualize the complete picture. This is an essential part of your art training.

After having followed the above instructions, take up a medium hard pencil and draw very lightly the essential lines of the subject you have selected. If you start drawing with heavy black lines, you kill your vision of the picture. Not only are these mistakes impressed on the paper, but they are also impressed on the mind. After having lightly sketched in your study in proper proportion and balance, start to draw accurately and with vision. Above all, do not sacrifice accuracy to speed. Haste is liable to produce errors which make corrections and erasures necessary and mar the pleasure derived from the study of art.

Try to draw pictures of your own invention in order to cultivate creative ability. It would be beneficial to discover how well you can redraw a picture from memory without having recourse to the original copy. After sufficient practice in memory drawing, try drawing directly from nature.

Drawing teaches the eye to observe and the hand to coordinate with the mind. Training your hand and mind to coordinate gives quite a thrill when it is mastered. Without order and method, your work will be uneven in quality.

When starting a picture, it is well not to get interested in detail too soon. The most forcible style is maintained by keeping the whole drawing under way, rather than by finishing in detail one part at a time. The first line in a drawing should be the most important and the last of least value. The problems are somewhat different in each picture, but this makes one of the fascinating aspects of the study of art.

PERSPECTIVE

Perspective is the principle by which an object receding from the position of the viewer appears, to the viewer, smaller than its true size, and, conversely, an object approaching the viewer's position seems more and more to approximate its true size. The knowledge of perspective is an indispensable aid to the artist, who must represent on a flat surface subjects which, in actuality, exist in three dimensional space. As a test, take a ruler and measure a person forty feet away. As he approaches, see how much larger he seems to become. The test shows the apparent variation in size of an object, depending on its remoteness from or nearness to the viewer.

The vanishing point is that point on the horizon where parallel lines (perspective lines) seemingly converge and terminate. The vanishing point is always on the horizon. Any object within a picture will have perspective lines, through these lines are not visible in the finished drawing.

The horizon line is always on a level with the eyes of the observer, and it changes with the observer's changing positions, as shown in the drawings that follow.

The drawings in this book have been chosen to illustrate the variety of problems which the artist encounters when creating a picture. Study them carefully and then apply the principles which they present when next you make a sketch.

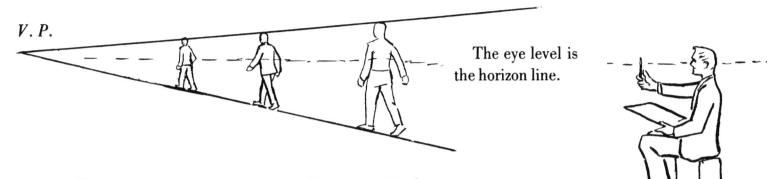

V. P.

The eye level is
the horizon line.

Here, the exercise is measuring the apparently de-
creasing size of a figure as it grows distant from the
viewer's position.

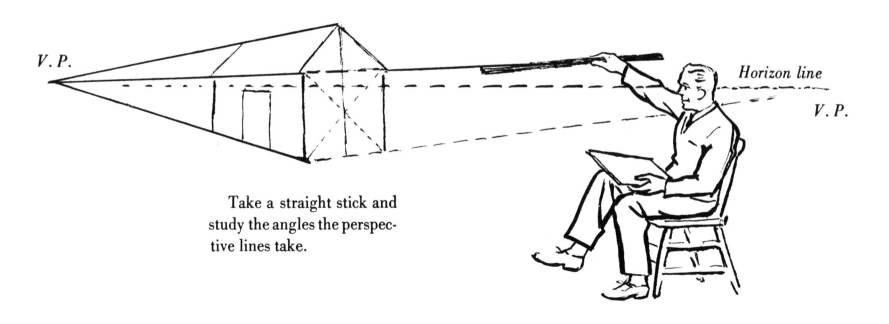

V. P.

Horizon line

V. P.

Take a straight stick and
study the angles the perspective lines take.

The tracks are parallel with each other; the poles are all the same height. As they grow distant to the eyes, the rails appear closer to each other, and the poles appear smaller, until they reach a vanishing point.

V. P.

Horizon line

The center of each mat is obtained by drawing a line from corner to corner. The center is where the lines cross. This exercise helps in getting the foreshortening of the figures on the mats, because the figures, even though they may not appear to be, are also divided in half. It can be seen that the top half seems smaller than the bottom half.

V.P. V.P. V.P.

Horizon line

Studies in foreshortening

SHADING TECHNIQUES

Practice the above strokes, trying to achieve their weight and keeping the members in each group separated by approximately equal distances. Whether you are right-handed or left-handed, you will find this excellent practice.

 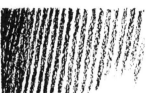 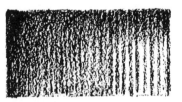 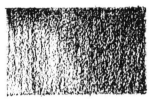 

Now keep your lines closer together, melting them into flat tints and graded tints, as illustrated above. Practice this shading until you are proficient in controlling the various pressures you can apply to a pencil.

Sharpen the lead of a BBB pencil so that it resembles a chisel; wear the lead smooth for the broad strokes. The pencil then will prove practical and effective for sketching. You can lend interest to a drawing by varying the width of your strokes. The foreground can usually be treated with broader and darker strokes than the background, which is usually light.

LIGHT AND SHADOW

When light falls on any object, it makes a shadow. These sketches show how shadows are cast from a single source of light, such as a lantern, a reading lamp, a spotlight.

 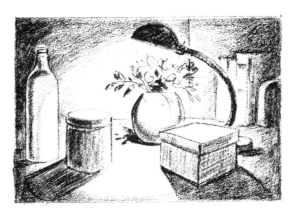 

If you draw a picture of an outdoor scene, the sun or the moon is your source of light.

Long late-afternoon shadows   **Short midday shadows**   **Moonlight—strong contrast**

FLOWERS

Long-stemmed flowers can be cut to varying lengths to avoid crowding in a vase. Too many flowers in one grouping prove to be unwieldy. When arranging flowers in a vase as well as when drawing them, aim at a rhythmic, balanced design.

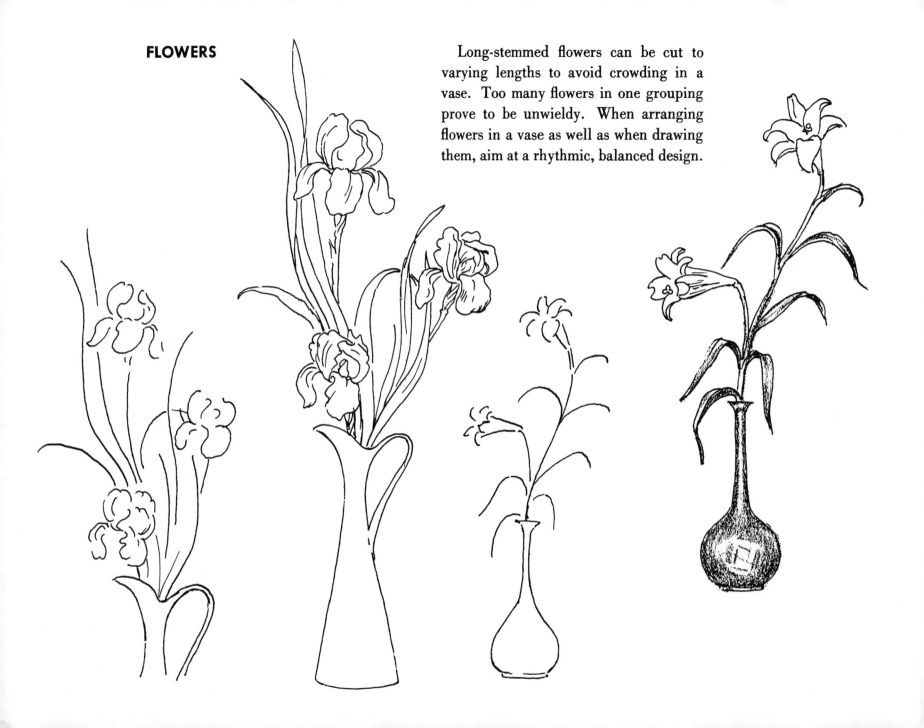

Place the long lines
first, and fill in later.

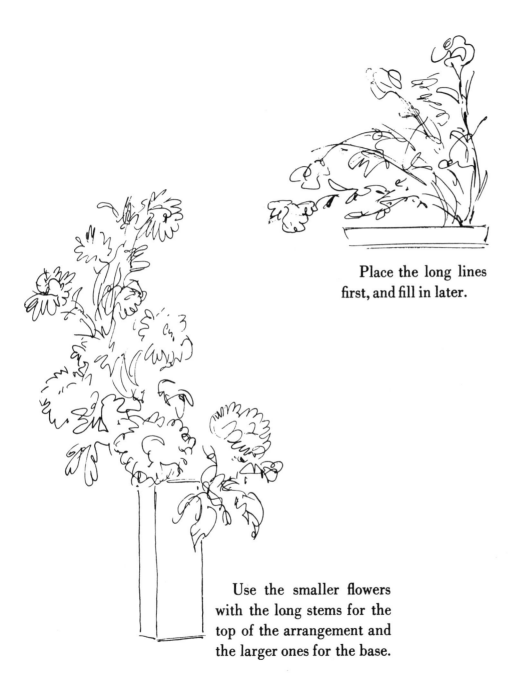

Use the smaller flowers
with the long stems for the
top of the arrangement and
the larger ones for the base.

Preliminary sketch

It is a good practice to
make a rough sketch of the
proposed grouping. A few
preliminary lines will save a
lot of fussing.

A drawing well prepared is half done.

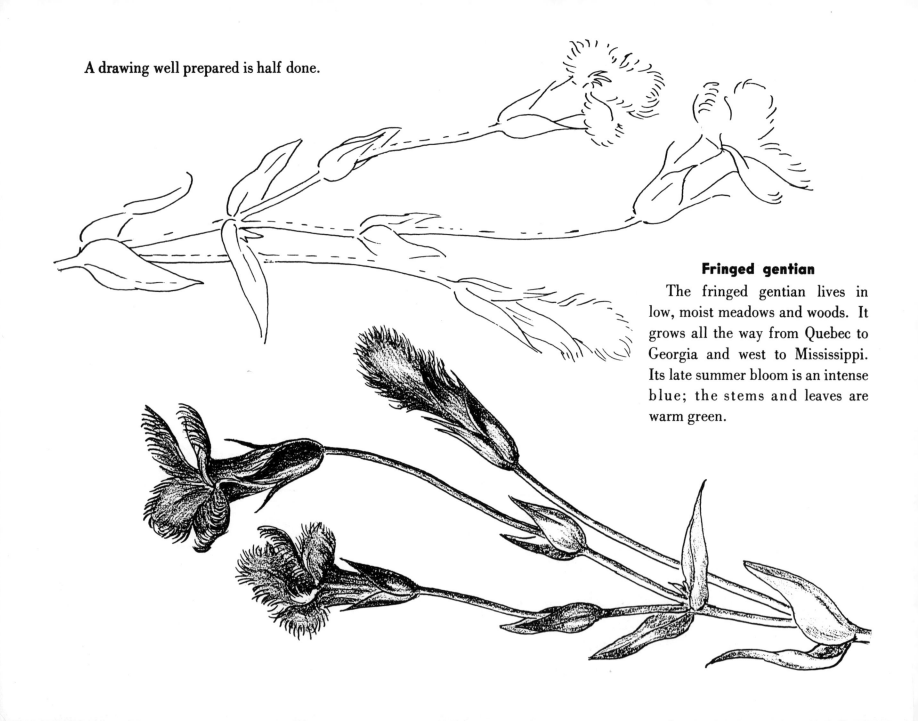

Fringed gentian

The fringed gentian lives in low, moist meadows and woods. It grows all the way from Quebec to Georgia and west to Mississippi. Its late summer bloom is an intense blue; the stems and leaves are warm green.

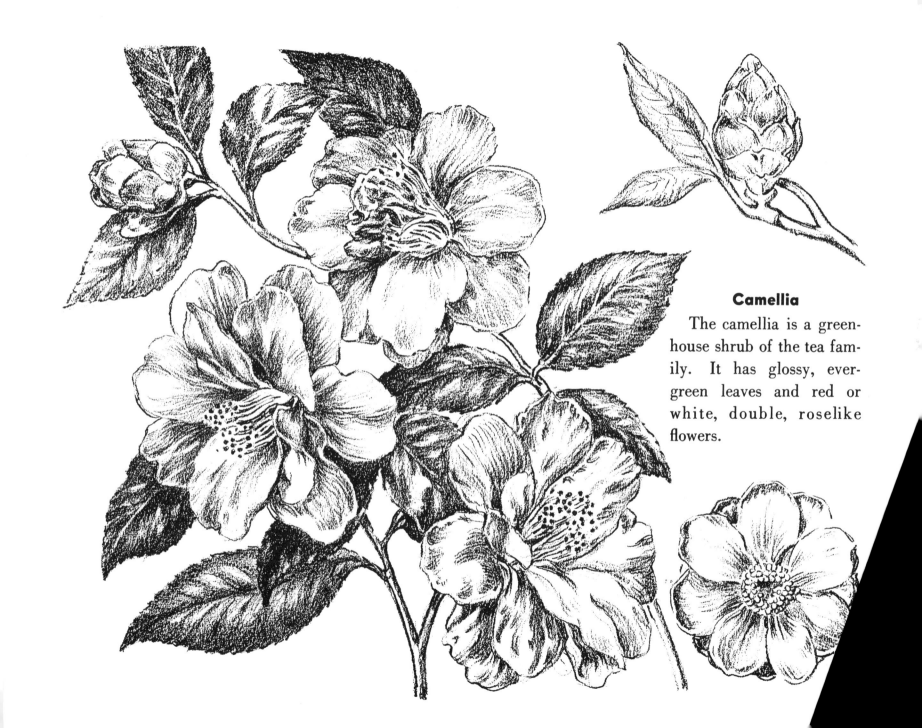

Camellia

The camellia is a greenhouse shrub of the tea family. It has glossy, evergreen leaves and red or white, double, roselike flowers.

Fundamental Outline

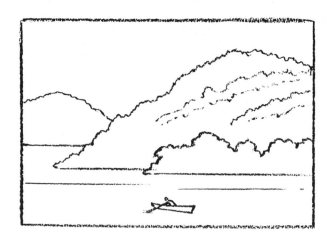

The first and all-important concern of the sketcher is learning to see the forms of his subject in simple outline; he must avoid interest in details when only making quick sketches. Details can be added later, when the artist is elaborating his sketches into finished drawings or paintings.

Shading the background of landscapes with vertical strokes gives it a feeling of solidity. Here, such shading keeps the mountains in simple masses.

The mountain in the far background is silhouetted and shows no detail other than a slightly broken line that indicates trees on the mountain top.

The broken line is also used on the nearer mountain but with detail. This mountain is shaded to suggest that it is covered with trees in the distance, middle distance, and foreground.

The group of trees on the right is obviously nearer than that on the left so the shapes of the shadows made by the foliage are shown. These shapes should be planned in such a way as to achieve a good design, whether they exist that way in nature or not.

Quick Sketches

Sketch books filled with small draw
ings that take only five or ten minutes
complete are valuable. Such sketches tea
an artist to make quick decisions on
selection and composition of sub
Many subjects for later elaboration
noted down when they first presen
selves to view. They might othe
passed by because of lack of tim

Valuable ideas for future reference can be stored up by filling notebooks with such quick impressions. Use a very soft pencil, the best medium when speed is required.

The early morning haze creates a chance for working in flat tints without much detail in the massed groupings. This sketch was made with a soft pencil on a grained paper.

This picture of the old stone bridge treats the problem in masses of flat tints with much paper showing, but in defined shapes. The white areas should not be pencilled.

Lake Louise, Canadian Rockies

Calm sea

Turbulent sea

Waves breaking on a beach

Golden Gate Strait at sunset

Drawing such a scene as that above requires patience and should be worked on when the artist is in a quiet mood. The procedure followed in the layout of this drawing was first to place the horizon line, next to outline the clouds and fix the sun, then to sketch in the surrounding hills, and finally to work on the ripples of the water. The shading was done in the same sequence.

DRAWING THE FIGURE

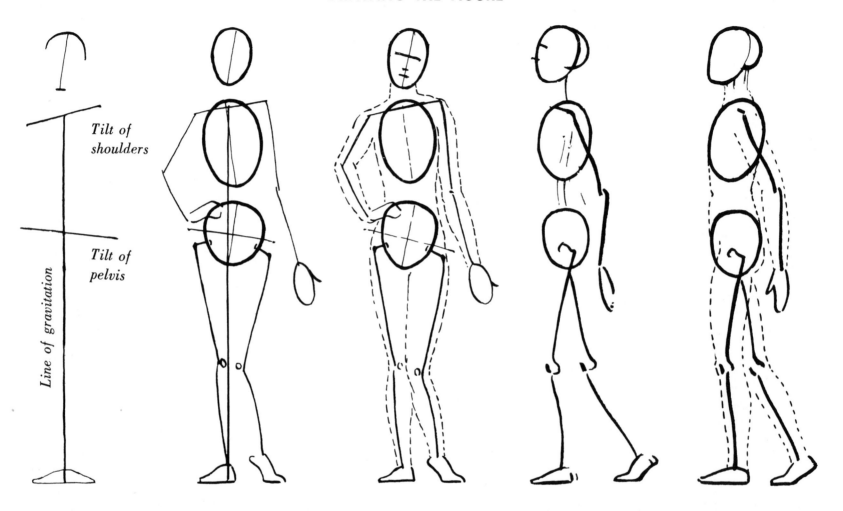

First, draw a perpendicular line to indicate the placement of the figure. This is the balance line, or *line of gravitation*. Next, indicate the action of the shoulders by a horizontal line. Leave enough room above the shoulder line for the neck and head. Draw a second horizontal line to indicate the tilt of the pelvis.

Use egg shapes for the start of the head, the torso, and the pelvis. Egg shapes help the eye to judge proportions. In the two figures at left, most of the weight rests on the right leg, which forces the pelvis and shoulders to tilt in opposite directions. The foot touches the line of gravitation.

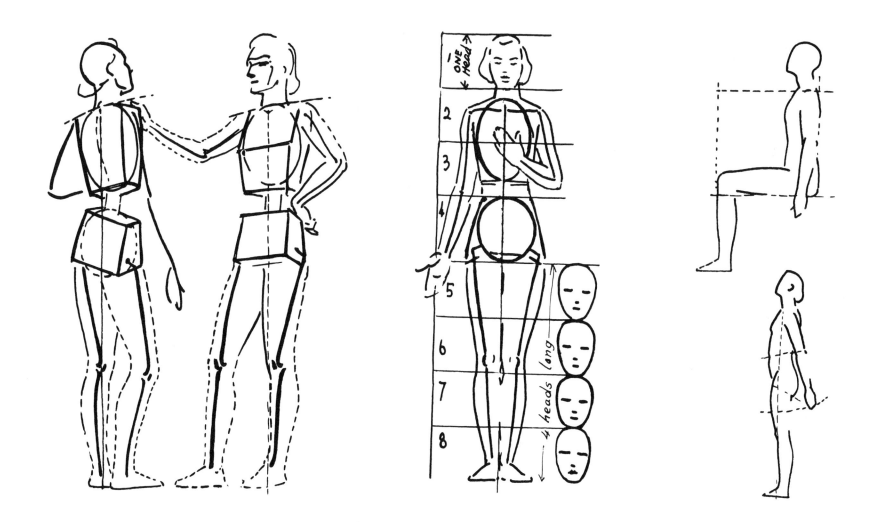

Draw stick figures lightly. Add some of the anatomy, referring to the anatomy pages ahead.

The neck is lower in front than in the back. A man's chin is often on a level with the back of his collar. At every turn of the head, neck-muscle forms change. In a back view, start the line of gravitation at the base of the neck (the prominent vertebra).

The average fashion figure is 8 heads high. Study the proportioned figure above. Note that breast line is 2 heads down; navel is 3 heads down. The hand reaches the middle of the thigh. The distance from shoulder to seat equals that from knee to back.

Practice drawing the stick figures and simplified skeleton sketches on these pages until you can draw them from memory. This will help train the eye to observe proportions and expressions of figures in action.

Originate stick and skeleton figures in other poses.

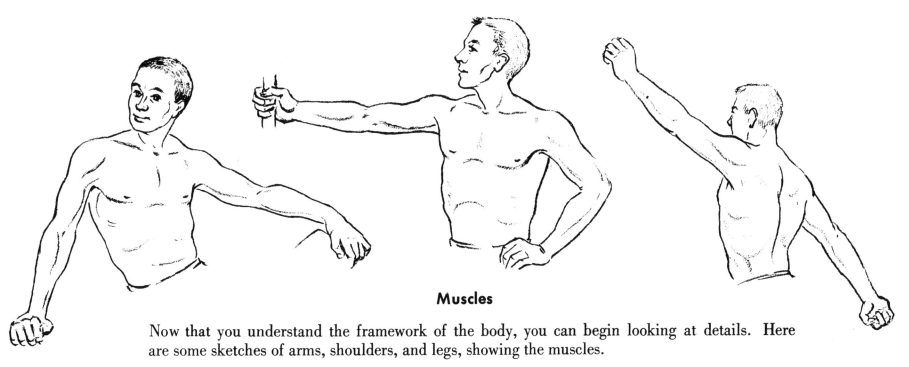

Muscles

Now that you understand the framework of the body, you can begin looking at details. Here are some sketches of arms, shoulders, and legs, showing the muscles.

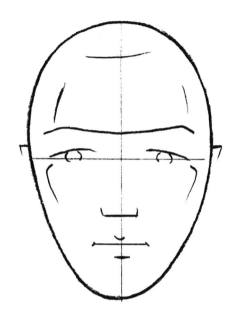

Heads and Faces

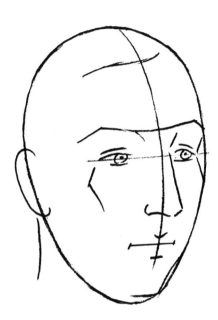

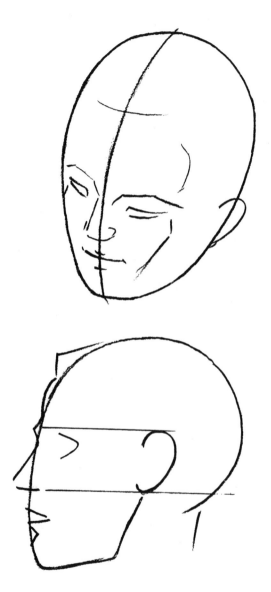

Basic Lines

Use the oval to start the general outline of a head. It helps to indicate the size and position desired. Draw the facial line down the front of the face, then the line of the eyes about midway between the chin and top of head. Draw a line for the base of the nose; divide the space between the nose and chin into three parts;and place the mouth one third from the nose.

The basic lines are not as soft as in a woman's face. Remember, the hat (crown) fits the head.

Arms

Observe and draw the arm in various positions. Note how its contours change with each new position.

Hands

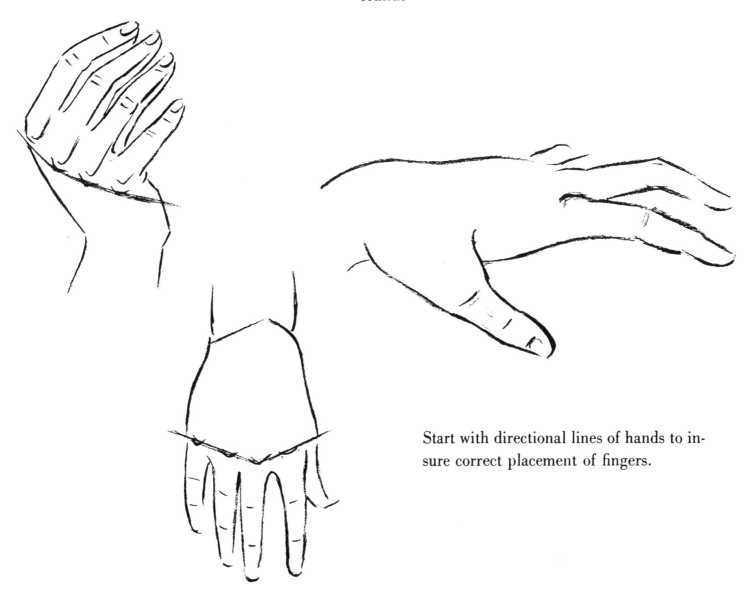

Start with directional lines of hands to insure correct placement of fingers.

Legs

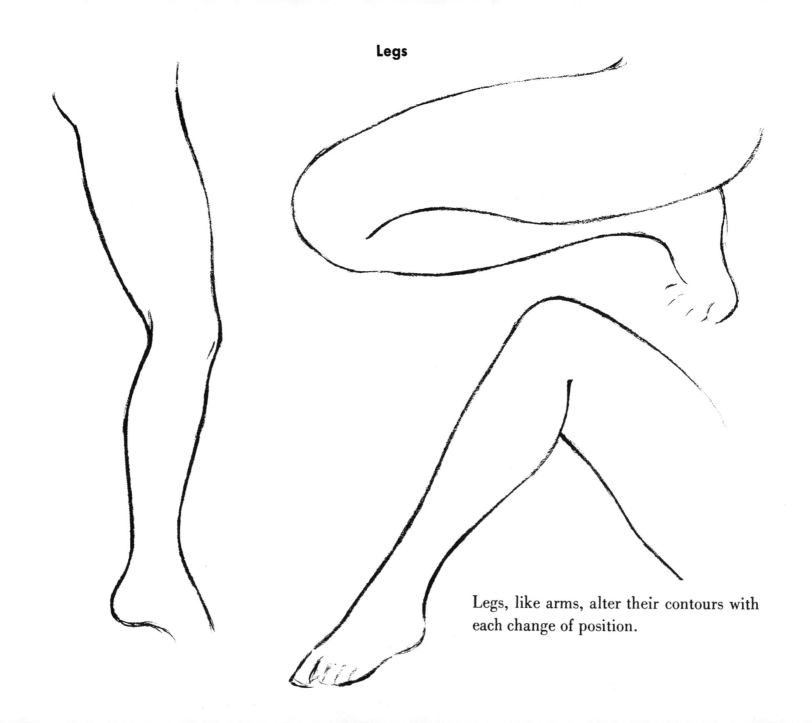

Legs, like arms, alter their contours with each change of position.

Shading

Start with directional lines. Next, draw a contour of the figure. Finally, block in masses of shading.

DRAWING ANIMALS

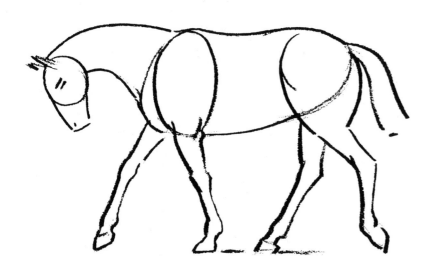

Walking

Trotting

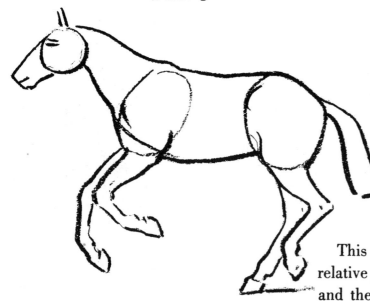

Cantering

This page represents the relative positions of the legs and the feet of a horse in various gaits.

Galloping

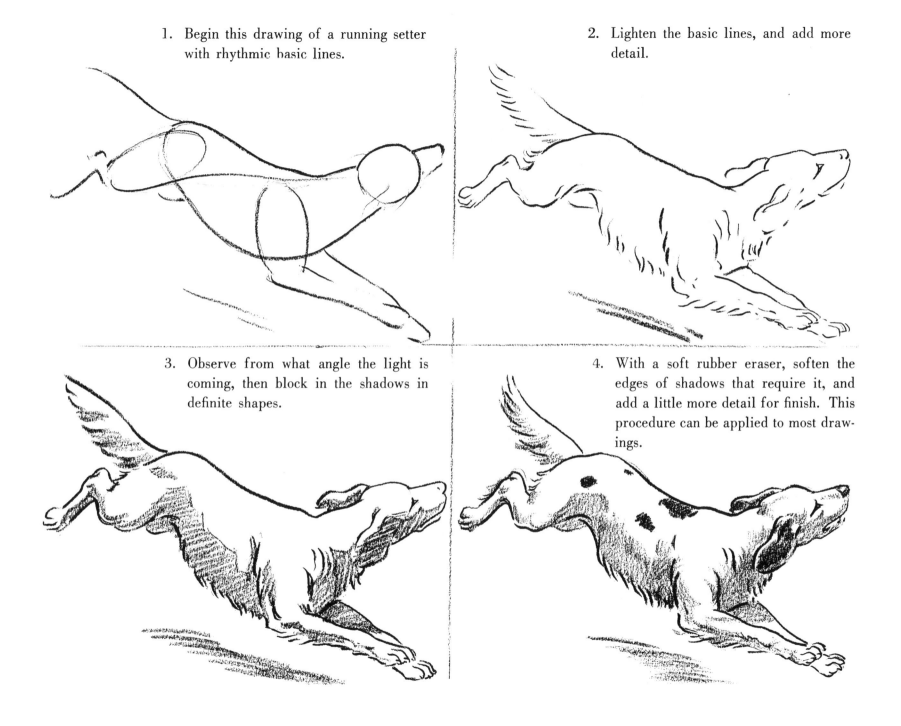

1. Begin this drawing of a running setter with rhythmic basic lines.

2. Lighten the basic lines, and add more detail.

3. Observe from what angle the light is coming, then block in the shadows in definite shapes.

4. With a soft rubber eraser, soften the edges of shadows that require it, and add a little more detail for finish. This procedure can be applied to most drawings.

Tabby Cat

Contour sketching

Brush drawings

Basic circular lines

Ordinary writing ink is fine for
brush drawings.

Basic lines

Lamb

Old goat

Young goat

Practice making your own grouping of
sheep and goats.

Squirrels

Stick to your basic lines and then build on them. If your sketches are poor, it is because you have not used enough basic lines.

If sketching from nature, do not change your drawing every time your subject moves. It will often return to the original pose.

Basic lines

Rabbit

Beaver

Hare

To have character a pencil line must be made with a soft pencil. Hard pencils have little feeling of touch, but are useful for starting a drawing.

Raccoon

Polar bears

In order to learn expressions and proportions, get a good outline first. Do not shade any more than is really necessary. Shading is less important than outline.

African leopards

Jaguar foot print

Jaguar's muscular system

Jaguar

The man-eating jaguar is found all the way from southwest Texas to Central America and Patagonia. In color and skin pattern it seems to be related to the old world leopard. The jaguar is a much heavier animal than the African leopard.

Stalking his prey

Tiger

The royal Bengal tiger of India is the most beautiful member of the cat family. It is of enormous size, over three feet high and weighing from 600 to 800 pounds.

Practice drawing the head in different positions.

Muscular system

Lion cub

African lion

In size it may measure ten feet from the tip of the nose to the tip of the tail. Study the muscular system on this page before starting to draw one of these lions. Try to find the basic lines before attempting to finish the drawing.

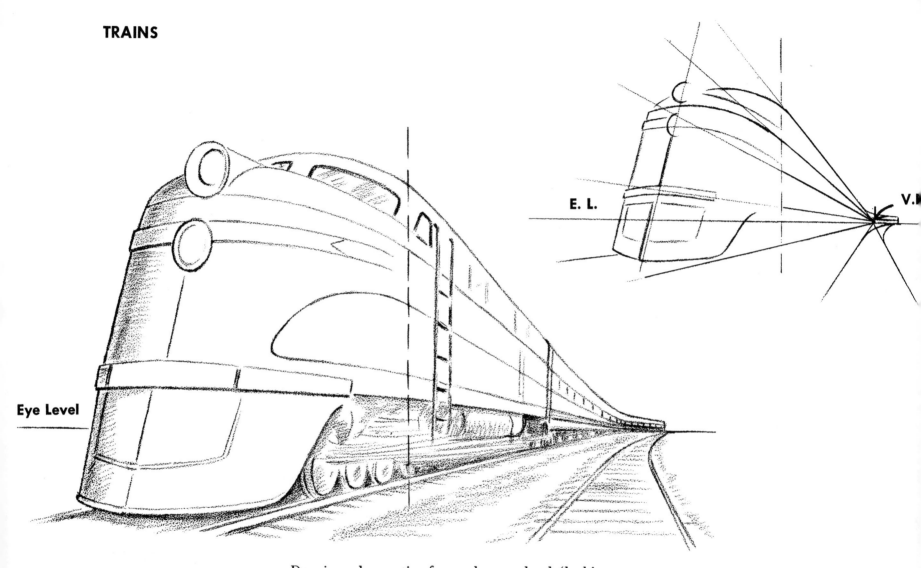

E. L.

V.

Eye Level

Drawing a locomotive from a low eye level (looking up
at it) makes it appear big and powerful. The end of the
train disappears at the vanishing point (refer to the section
on *Perspective*).

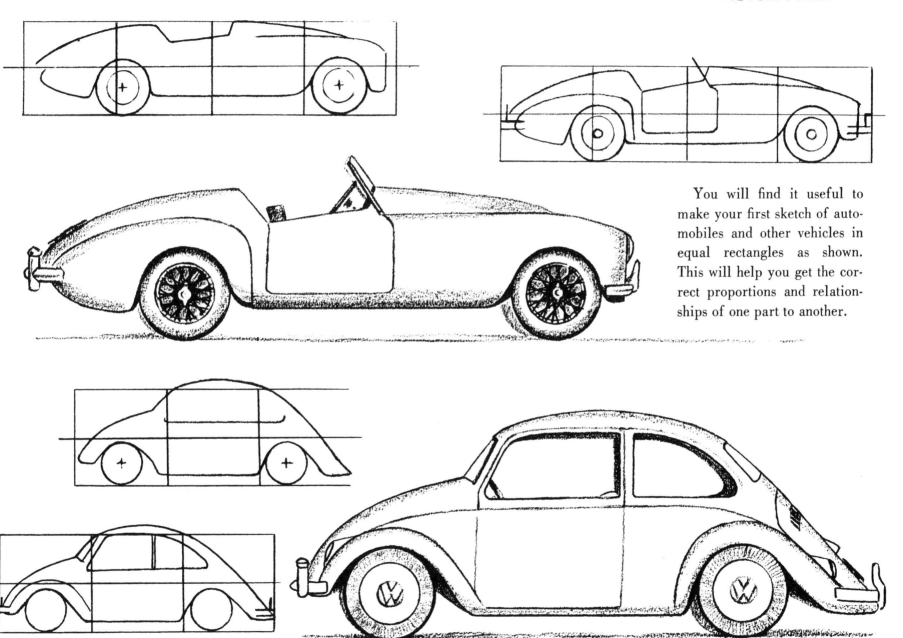

You will find it useful to make your first sketch of automobiles and other vehicles in equal rectangles as shown. This will help you get the correct proportions and relationships of one part to another.

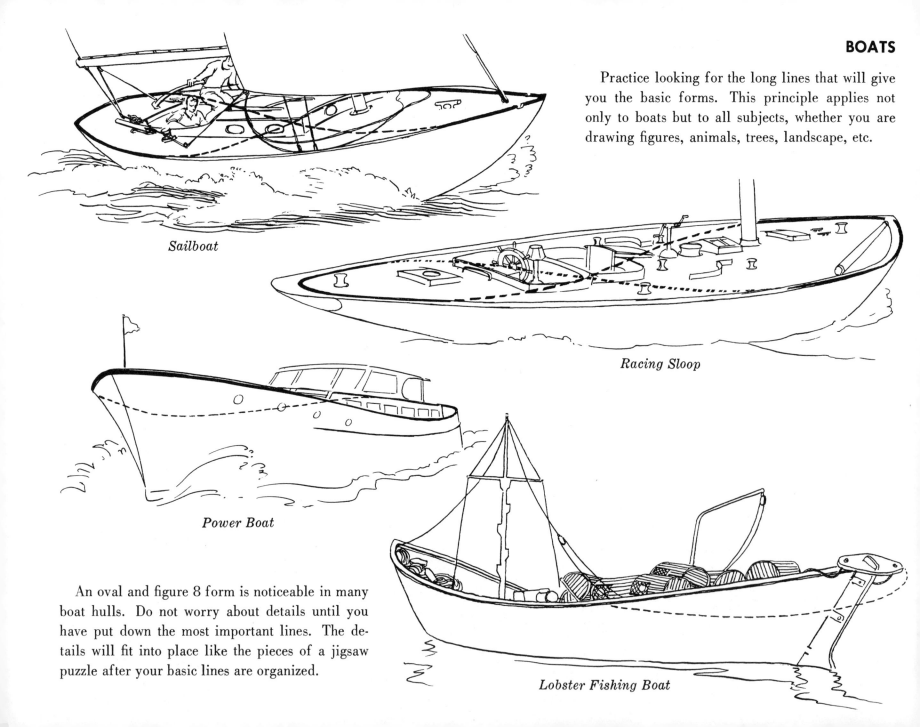

Practice looking for the long lines that will give you the basic forms. This principle applies not only to boats but to all subjects, whether you are drawing figures, animals, trees, landscape, etc.

Sailboat

Racing Sloop

Power Boat

An oval and figure 8 form is noticeable in many boat hulls. Do not worry about details until you have put down the most important lines. The details will fit into place like the pieces of a jigsaw puzzle after your basic lines are organized.

Lobster Fishing Boat

A marine subject is usually more suited to a horizontal than a vertical picture, due to the long line of the horizon. Action is shown by diagonal lines, with the boat and its sails tilted to one side. The swirling lines of the water give the effect of movement caused by the wind.

The Bluenose schooner shown here has a noticeable figure 8 in its deck line.

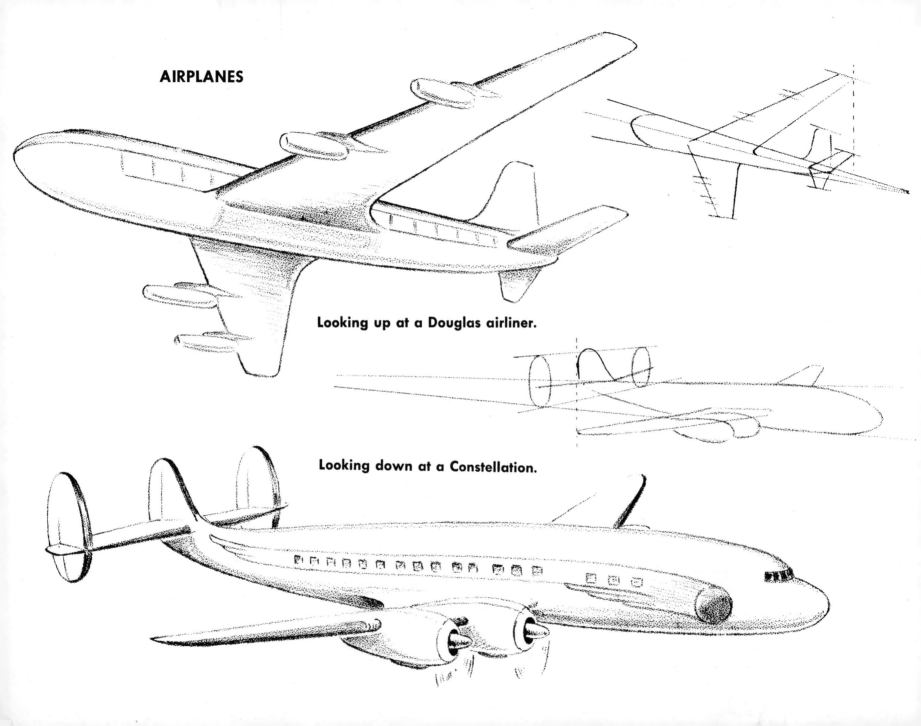

AIRPLANES

Looking up at a Douglas airliner.

Looking down at a Constellation.